WHAT IS IT LIKE?
Lidija Dimkovska

Translated from the Macedonian by
Ljubica Arsovska, Patricia Marsh and Peggy Reid

WHAT IS IT LIKE?
Lidija Dimkovska

All rights reserved. No part of this book may be reproduced, stored in a retrieval system or transmitted in any form or by any means electronic, mechanical, photocopying, recording or otherwise, without the prior permission of the publisher.

ISBN 978-1903110829

First published in this edition 2022 by Wrecking Ball Press.

Copyright: Lidija Dimkovska

Cover design: humandesign.co.uk

All rights reserved.

ACKNOWLEDGEMENTS:

Grateful acknowledgment is due the editors of the following magazines, in which these poems first appeared in English:

Asymptote: Punctuation of Life
Benington Review: Emptiness, Do you feel dizzy?
Columbia Journal: Freedom, A Letter from Prison, Going back, Chopin's Heart
Exquisite Corpse: Wannsee Diptych, Rubbish, What is it like
Los Angeles Review: Hump, Behind the Door, Summa Summarum
Macedonian PEN Review in English: The Crumbling World
Plume: New Home
Poetry International: Asylum Seekers
Rochford Street Review: Echo
Sand: What is it like
Solstice: At the Last Judgement, Deathbed Poem
Struga Poetry Evenings: The Past Indefinite
Times Literary Supplement: The Pet
World Literature Today: Without Me, A Curse, Traduttore, traditore

For Ema and Aleš, here and now

*My daughter's baby teeth come loose in one country,
fall out in another,
and her new teeth grow in a third country.*

*At the same time, we are alive at one end of the world,
dead at another,
and already immortal at the third.*

*There are expendable, surplus ones in the world,
Who don't appear on the horizon
(Not figuring in your files,
Their home being the dumping grounds).*
(Marina Tsvetaeva, "The Poet")

*How mixed up our times have become –
it makes your hair stand on end!*
(Blaže Koneski, "A Midnight Dialogue")

CONTENT

from IN BLACK AND WHITE

I. SUMMA SUMMARUM

What is it like?	15
My Grave	17
Hump	18
Behind the Door	20
New Home	22
At the Last Judgement	24
Summa Summarum	26

II. CORRESPONDENCE WITH THE WORLD

Wannsee Diptych	29
Rubbish	33
Deathbed Poem	35
A Letter from Prison	36
Without Me	37
Correspondence With the World	38

III. PUNCTUATION OF LIFE

Freedom	43
Journey	45
Going back	47
Chopin's Heart	48
Echo	50
Asylum Seekers	51
Punctuation of Life	53

from BOUNDARY SITUATION

I. BETWEEN TOMORROW AND YESTERDAY

The Past Indefinite 59
The Watch 61
Suitcases 62
Behind the Dead 64
Emptiness 66
Women Customs Officers 67
Do You Feel Dizzy? 69
Plus-minus 71

II. CRUMBLING

The Crumbling House 75
The Crumbling Memory 76
The Crumbling Country 78
The Crumbling History 79
The Crumbling Future 81
The Crumbling World 83

III. A HUMAN OR HUMANKIND?

The Pet 87
Traduttore, traditore 89
A Curse 91
A Human or Humankind? 92
The (Dis)comfort of Existence 94
Whose are You? 96
Cleaning 98
Means of Transport 100
The Evil 102
History 104

from IN BLACK AND WHITE

I. SUMMA SUMMARUM

What is it like?

to be a child of parents killed in war,
to be a child of parents who've divorced,
or an African child on a jumbo poster,
to live in an institution for the handicapped,
to have a key to a social housing flat,
to receive aid in the form of flour, oil,
sanitary towels and cotton buds,
to have a bone marrow transplant donation bank account in
your name,
to live in an SOS Village with a Big Mother of nine children
and an auntie who comes once a week to iron clothes and play
cards,
to sleep in a cardboard box in front of the parliament
or in the subway of a metropolis hosting a summit meeting,
to be a doll in a traditional costume
instead of a traffic policeman at the crossroads,
what is it like when children adopt parents, and not the other
way round,
to down blood quickly before it oxidises,
to be the thyroid gland of the family politics,
to be with people who make you drool,
and others who give you a lump in the throat,
to keep the softest towel for the visitor from abroad,
and the hardest bed for the suicide who has survived,
to be a splinter in God's eye,
to gather knowledge in a teaspoon of sticky syrup,
to have views like washed stockings
that cannot find their pairs,
to feel that neither your skin nor the homeland fit you any
more,
to hang on a monastery lime tree

the man who was the last to kiss you on the brow,
to be the topical issue in a low-budget film,
to have a belly button that draws in before the tongue,
and the tongue before the live measure of the spirit,
to become a tenant of your own existence,
to become aware that life is a non-swimmer's game
with waves higher than oneself?

My Grave

Every day I watch my grave in the garden
included in the price of the house,
with a board over the hole,
with a tombstone of white limestone,
with a photograph in a gold frame,
and the year of birth separated by a dash
from the empty space for death.
The grave is there under the pear tree facing the house,
staring at me even when I have my back turned to it.
In spring the cats loosen the board,
and sparrows in the tree shit on it for good luck,
in summer an occasional overripe pear
chips off a piece of the tombstone,
in autumn the rain thins its spine, bites its figure,
in winter the snow rams it deeper into the ground.
It's the focal point of every thunderbolt,
of every earthquake the epicentre.
It crumbles, decays, decomposes,
it's becoming ever smaller, more wizened, brought to its knees,
the grave is disappearing before my eyes,
it's falling into its own hole, turning from dust to dust.
I look at it this morning, what's left of it is no more
than a small pile of limestone being scattered by the wind,
broken shards of board big enough to build nesting boxes,
and the photo in its gold frame
flutters around the from – to.
My grave is vanishing faster and faster,
just like my life.

Hump

In front of me a man is pushing
a barrow full of empty plastic bottles.
The path is narrow, I can't overtake him.
I follow him, watch him.
Worn-out trousers,
furrowed hands,
a pair of mismatched slippers,
and under the ragged T-shirt
    – a hump, marked with pain
as with a Star of David.
He's the same age as me,
of a time long past.
In vain has he memorised
the short poems about the fatherland,
unnecessary like theory learned by heart
but never put into practice in this world
where today he has
neither father nor fatherland.
Has someone underwritten his life
in black and white,
or do only these bottles rate him among the living?
The bottles bounce,
he leans into the rhythm of the barrow,
I hear his stomach rumble,
and a sigh escape his mouth.
The path is long, we tread one behind the other,
I in the beat of his gait,
he in the cadence of the three wheels.
I feel that out of my heavy-heartedness,
from the uneasiness of my senses,

hope, future and aim evaporate,
the liquids leach out of my organs,
the air is squeezed out, my weight dissipates,
I no longer have content,
I'm turning into an empty plastic bottle
that gets smaller and smaller and then throws itself
among the other bottles,
I take the least room in the cart,
and the man, sinking into his own deepest place,
only now begins to sweat,
wipes his face first with one hand then with the other
while the barrow topples
and he stops, takes off his T-shirt
and dabs the streams of sweat running down his neck,
turns his head left and right,
but sees no one behind him,
only the tip of his own hump,
marked with pain as with the Star of David.

Behind the Door

When I took the gun off the nail,
the cracked plaster behind the door crumbled,
an imprint of emptiness opened up in the patch.
How many people can one kill with it?
And how many without pressing the trigger?
In a dream, or with a curse, with a leer
or with eyes to the ground, without a word?
With a sneer, with poisonous laughter,
with a swearword, with a thought, with a forethought?
How do the snipers from the last war
spend the peacetime?
I disarmed myself, buried the gun in the ground.

Then I hung Dürer's hare behind the door,
stuffed, with a small mirror around its neck.
The draught in the house
turned it now to the door now to the patch,
like a pendant hanging from the rear-view mirror,
and it kept beating itself in the little mirror
believing it was hitting another little hare.
In its dream all people were hares,
and all hares people. They waged wars with my gun
till sunrise, undecided, but with casualties.

One day I found my front door gone,
someone had taken it away with him, to his grave or to the market.
Cracked and crumbled the wall gaped,
no gun, no hare, no past.
What else could I hang on it
but the little purse with the key without a keyhole,

with basil tucked in its bow,
and under it a calendar with no year
with tombstone photos
of us all, neither alive nor kicking.

New Home

This house has no prehistory,
it hasn't belonged to anyone before us,
there's no title-deed, or ghosts, or ancestors,
no one's conscience in the corners exuding carbon dioxide,
no one's shadow looming above the stairs,
it smells of nothing and no one in the hall.
Behind each open drawer gapes an abyss,
no wedged letters peep, no bills or photos,
the keyholes make a factory-fresh sound,
no one has made the floor creak or hum yet.
This place is still public, its genes are still new,
happiness is not hereditary, but unhappiness is,
and only we can be the first hapless ones here.
Children always leave every home,
and then the home adopts new children,
but this house itself is adopted,
with time before us like an open ticket that costs a lot.
Our waking lives slowly loosen their grip
as we sleep every night in a different room,
we fall on the mattresses, their labels still on,
like the temperature in the radiators
we flow out through the siphon of moving house into clean
                                                                  drains,
we mark the days of the present
as if waiting for a soldier to come home,
for the home, each day that passes is a reservoir filling with
                                                                   memories,
each person who enters it a deliverer of a future.
Our cases and boxes are unpacked,
the furniture fills with the breath of human objects,

our own smell slowly inhabits the hall
and we open the door more often,
the space takes on the shape of our bodies,
our feet pad the floor, the parquet creaks,
crumbs under the table, a doll's arm under the bed,
a paper on the doorstep, a swing bin like in any house,
instead of an alarm – life and death stand guard.
I never looked for a way out, only a way in,
little knowing that it's an interior without draught,
without a frozen mirror,
the peacefulness of a baby wrapped in a blanket,
life teeming with everyday events,
home, pH neutral history.

At the Last Judgement

You, who were so alive,
why did you, against my will,
move to the world of the dead?

In time
my wife stopped loving me,
my child hugging me,
my dog fawning on me,
my neighbour greeting me,
my brother visiting me,
my sister calling me,
my friend understanding me,
my fatherland respecting me,
my freedom delighting me,
You answering my prayers.

For a while
I went on loving my wife,
hugging my child,
patting my dog,
greeting my neighbour,
visiting my brother,
calling my sister,
understanding my friend
respecting my fatherland,
delighting in my freedom,
praying to You.

But after a while I, too,
stopped loving my wife,
hugging my child,
patting my dog,
greeting my neighbour,
visiting my brother,
calling my sister,
understanding my friend
respecting my fatherland,
enjoying my freedom,
praying to You.

My world and your world
were divided by a tombstone.
Under it now and then I sense
someone up there sobbing, lighting a candle for me,
but I don't know which one of you it is.

Summa Summarum

It takes nine months for the foetus
to develop into a human being.
And then a childhood, youth and old age
to be one.
And whether it will develop into a human being worthy of the name
no one can tell.
A whole life might not prove long enough
to become a proper person.
And it takes just a second for a body
to turn into a corpse.
You live for yourself, and die for others
so they can't live without you.
Even when forgiven with good
evil is remembered as evil.
But good is never remembered for good
turned into evil.
You can wash your face a hundred times,
but never your honour.
When washing your face you wet your sleeves,
and rubbing clean your honour soaks your conscience.
You need soap and water for your face,
your honour needs the conscience of the blood.
And now
who will gloat more:
The Nobody and Nothing who has become Something
or the Something that Nobody and Nothing
has turned into?

II. CORRESPONDENCE WITH THE WORLD

Wannsee Diptych

Of course I can tell you what Eichmann said then
because I heard it with my own ears, and when somebody talks
                                          about food
I remember it all, word for word. They say it's my professional
                                          deformation,
although I'd risen from cook in the kitchen to housekeeper
                               serving coffee to important guests.
I can still see him, straining forward, anxious
to prevent the chair from creaking, and then it usually creaks
                                                   louder,
his hand measuring the precise two spans between his coffee cup
and the table edge while his glance measured the others,
and as I placed the last cup on the table,
he said: "Gentlemen, this may sound banal, perhaps,
but this morning, as I was having my breakfast of butter and
                                      jam, I actually realised
what the Jew is for our Reich. The Jew, gentlemen, is a creation
                                    made of empty calories,"
he said, and leaned on his elbow between the cup and the edge
                                    of the dining table,
overlooking Großer Wannsee,
legibly completing the protocol of 20th January '42.
"He's like potato crisps," he said, "like American hamburgers,
                                      or chocolate,
filling our nation with fats that are harmful to our blue veins,
the same in Poland or Albania, in millions or counted on the
                                                  fingers,
he's a wolf in sheep's clothing, muddying the water for our
                                      holy shepherd."
And while the heads around nodded like fortune-tellers reading
                                          coffee grounds

with a flourish Eichmann signed his name to the mass graveyard
of Europe.
I stood in the doorway and peered with lowered eyes at the
bellies of those present,
breathing peacefully under their fat – a living measure of life.
His was the only bony body; his face glazed with ice
had neither blood nor conscience. Who could love a man like
that, I thought,
wiping my hands on my apron, but I couldn't wipe them clean.
"Ah, if only you knew what's being done there," the villa's
victualler whispered to me in the kitchen,
"there," he said, his finger pointing to Hell, "that is where all the
Jews are,
ribs covered with striped rags, that is the necropolis of the world.
And no one will return to life, not even if they live to be a hundred."

I have lived to be a hundred. My family have given me a telescope
so that I can bring the stars closer to me, and myself to the stars.
The morning after my birthday party I asked my eldest great
grandson
to take me to Wannsee. In the street, he started laughing. "Look,"
he said,
"it says 'Shut the gate. Danger wild boar' on the gate."
But that was another villa, once occupied by a young man with
red hair
who suddenly disappeared the night before the Conference.
When we got there, it smelled of grilled fish and sausages.
The lake captured the windowpanes in its mirrors. Adolescent
lovers
threw breadcrumbs to the ducks. The water
echoed like slaps. Two rabbis were leaving, pushing prams.

The latch on the gate clicked like a camera.
My great grandson pushed my wheelchair noiselessly
between the showerheads on hoses fixed to the walls. He winced.
"Earphones for the conscience," I whispered to him. "Listen
to how the world touched the bottom.
In '42 everything God had created was ruined for good.
And I was there. Housekeeper to the conference of evil. I served
                                                                                            coffee
to those who served the devil. In the kitchen I stared at
                                                                   Eichmann's coffee grounds
and do you know what I saw, son? A word in white letters. ENDE
                                                            in the middle of blackness.
The end of the world. It remained unrecognised. Yet with so
                                                                         many subtitles.
I didn't go home that night. Tears overcame me
in the first sheltered place near the villa. When I left
I had no intention of going back again.
All I wanted was to give birth, to give Germany different children,
To lighten the human conscience with angels of life, not of death."
Today my great grandchildren love potato crisps, American
                                                                    hamburgers and chocolate
more than anything else. And I don't say they can't have them.
They're always in a hurry to go somewhere if I start, "When I was
                                                                         young ..."
They go to Wannsee for picnics with boats and beer cans. They've
                                                              never set foot in the villa.
Only from a distance, as if they've just remembered something,
                                                                        they shout:
"Look, that's the villa where my great granny made coffee for the
                                                                           Nazis!"
And everyone looks amazed.

"And does she still remember what went on there?"
"Oh, yes. She's a hundred and no longer knows where she is and
                                        forgets our names,
but she remembers Wannsee. Down to the smallest detail.
Sometimes we're not sure who's riding in that wheelchair we push
– great granny or history."

Rubbish

You collect stickers and shells with your children,
and stamps and postcards,
arrange them devotedly in drawers and boxes,
smiling as your wife calls out
"You're only creating rubbish,"
not knowing that suddenly a day will come,
or rather the night of that day,
when you will be staggering blindly in your underwear
down the wet iron fire escape.
Tottering away from your home,
hands as empty as a new-dug grave
and fists black from beating the flames,
you dive beyond the diameter of God's will,
looking behind you, and they are not there, a distant cry and a
                                        profound silence.
Naked and small under the hose that brings you back to life,
while you shove it away,
to die is all you want, to expire under the blanket behind the
                                        hedge.
They are dead.

You drag yourself to the rubbish bin where you threw the last
                                        rubbish yesterday.
With numb fingers you rummage the stench, there, the green
                              plastic bag with the orange peel,
the silver paper from the chocolate you bought coming home
                                        from work,
the end of the last salami and the crushed cartons
the children drank their juice from before they went to bed:
all that is left of all of you, of your life where now you're alone.

You smell them, kiss them, and restore each peel to wholeness,
you gather the chocolate crumbs in the silver paper, the end of
>
> the salami
>
makes you dizzy with its familiar homeliness,
your children's last saliva is on the drinking-straws.
This green plastic bag of rubbish is all that is yours now.
You need to start again from the beginning, they tell you,
while you would know only how to start from the middle, how
>
> to change the old,
>
make it better, nicer, more loved.
But when the dead are no longer alive
nobody knows how to start from either the end or the beginning.
You know, you know very well, how life is turned into scraps
>
> of rubbish,
>
but not how these scraps of rubbish can be turned into life.

Deathbed Poem

What bed will I breathe my last on?
On some train, on some crossroads?
With the curtain up or down?
At noon or at dead of night?
Is it fate, a curse or good luck
to breathe your last with someone else there?
A part of the soul of the one to see me last alive
will depart together with mine.
With her dying breath my granny asked for a bite of pie,
my aunt bought herself the coat to be buried in,
which then hung on the hanger, tag on,
until they dressed her in it in death.
I will want half my grave to be there and half here.
The soul is breathed out in a moment of short circuit
when the fuses burn up and you are alone at home,
you fumble in the dark
to the end of the hall
where by the front door you push them back in their sockets,
the light flashes on and mows down your soul
while reality, blinded,
doesn't notice it, even though, behind your body,
it too wobbles towards its own hole.

A Letter from Prison

This prison allows letters
of up to four pages
every four months.
50 words a day.
1,500 a month. A lot? Too little?
Don't be so foolish as to write in them
about appeals to the court,
political moves,
financial calculations,
religious epiphanies,
sexual allusions,
coded secrets,
or mention weapons and drugs,
threats, plans,
escapes and attacks.
While you're here
write love letters only.
50 words a day.
1,500 a month,
four pages
every four months –
enough to tell all those dear to you
that you love them.
Once you're out of here
it's no longer our business
what you tell
the others.

Without Me

Like the automatic door on a train
my life closed.
Strangers remained on the platform,
but they each knew who they were waving to.
In the carriages – suitcases, hubbub,
passengers with their feet on the seats.
And one booked seat, by the window,
which everyone was eyeing from the corridor.
In the distance an old woman in black running for the train.
She fell exhausted on the grass
and the train left without her.
I pulled the red emergency brake.
The conductor crashed into me.
I pushed the door open and jumped out.
The train whistled, a shadow loomed through the windows.
The old woman in black was nowhere to be seen.
And my life left without me.

Correspondence with the World
to E.D.

Three drawers contain my entire correspondence with the world:
in the first—empty envelopes and stamps no longer valid
to the world I have never written to;
in the second—small self-addressed stamped envelopes
from the world that has written to me at my expense;
in the third—dust caught in spider's webs:
the only trace of the world that has never answered my letters.
And now, seated on the small chipboard chest,
as my ears burn I realise:
but of course I too am someone's conscience,
someone's first and last love,
someone must be talking about me,
and as others are in my dream I am in someone else's,
a prayer, a swear word, or a curse.
Many deaths are linked through my life,
I was an old child with wrinkles
and everything was clear to me, yet I understood nothing.
And now, when I myself have become a letter?
Not the full face but the profile is the essence, the self, the fate:
an ear, an eye, a nostril, a palm, a heel,
a kidney, lung, breast, ventricle.
There is no dialogue between couples, lookalikes,
the twenty-first century has alienated them. Individual men,
                                          individual women,
it's always their individual way even when the world
is one and only. There's no such post office where letters can be
                                                                  sent
that won't come back. Every correspondence

is an autopsy of thought.
World, you to whom I've written, who've written back to me or
                                                                                    not, you knew:
I have never wanted to get far,
but close,
as close as possible
to the most distant.

III. PUNCTUATION OF LIFE

Freedom

In the lift of the world
Freedom always presses the wrong button:
instead of on the ground floor she gets out in the basement
where masked robbers stand in front of the lift
who kick and slap her,
or grinning maniacs with their trousers down,
or security officers who pinch her bottom
when she turns back to the door of the lift,
which is already squeaking its way back up,
and then they all grab her by the breasts,
drag her by the legs, and she struggles,
beaten black and blue she drags herself up the stairs to the
                                                                               ground floor,
where children stand with their satchels
waiting for the lift to come down from the top floor.

"What *does* she look like!" they whisper,
then run up the stairs to their homes and lock the doors
                                                                               behind them,
afraid that Freedom might
lean against their door,
sprawl at their threshold,
ask them for water, bread or a bed.

And they don't know that the freedom they have in their life
is measured with the remaining cups from the tea set
in the Jewish museums across the world,
they don't know that the seas wash up people too, not just seashells,
they don't know that the executioner becomes a victim when
                                                                               he beheads her

and the victims become executioners when they forget her,
they don't know that the metal head of the hammer is always
                                                          loose
and falls off before the hammer is swung, straight onto your
                                                        fingers,
they don't know that it is that same freedom
they learn about in history classes,
but is easily run down by the train on the nearby railway,
they don't know that the freedom they have in their life
is a white surface over a black pit,
the same as the belly of a pregnant woman
that they too were born from,
but it is only in death
that some will also become free.

Journey

Time trampled on you the moment you set out.
In the coach across the border
the conductor wiped the seats
with a brochure on human rights someone left behind.
Rain didn't beat against the windows of the other passengers,
it was only yours that the raindrops hit like stones,
just like at the exit from a metro station you know
where it's always raining
and the little orphans sniff glue from plastic bags
sprawled on the escalators.
Your soul shivered in the buffer zone,
your body gaped like a cupboard emptied before moving out,
the night was the senselessness of the daytime sense.
You dreamt in snatches an unending dream of how
the nineteenth century travels around with a beard
like a drunk loser,
how the twentieth century has a haircut and a shave
at the town barber's,
and how the twenty-first runs frantically between the two.
In the first city the Politkovskaya Club awaits you
in the second – the Joyce Irish Pub,
in the third – white houses with lace curtains
and a notice: *Today is Dr Roberto's funeral.*
White underwear hung
from the balconies of Hell.
But Heaven's balconies
have long run out of clotheslines and pegs
to hang washed brains out to dry.
Grannies in the corners of the neighbourhood
didn't even hold out a hand any more.

On the table in the small room of your fellow countryman:
two volumes of *Das Kapital* and a key for the toilet.
An empty noose dangled from the ceiling light.
If everything is all right, one day
you too will become a postman here.
You'll unlock the town's cemetery
with a key from a big keyring
and read to the dead women
the letters from their dead husbands.
And then the neighbourhood boys
in their long black coats
will come upon you
and afterwards no one will
remember you any more,
not that you were here nor that you were born somewhere else.

Going Back

When you go back to your home town
you visit museums and galleries,
pause to listen to the buskers,
light candles in all the churches,
buy books by local authors
and the CDs by local bands
which have come out over the last six months,
treat yourself to some chocs from the town factory facing
                                                          bankruptcy,
make a detour to the outdoor market you haven't visited for a
                                                          long time,
meet friends for an hour or two
before going to a local film or theatre production
they're not interested in,

you do a lightning tour of your home town
in just a few days, drinking water from the bottle in your bag,
buying souvenir magnets and keyrings,
sitting on all the surviving benches
from your past,
turning down all the alleyways that have remained the same,
taking photos of the new buildings which look like warts,
mumbling to yourself, incomprehensible to everyone else,
when you go back to your home town
you realise you no longer have one,
that it has turned into a simple fact in a document,
Place of Birth, a point of birth and of no return.

Chopin's Heart

Chopin's heart in Warsaw –
walled up in the interior pillar of the church,
cannot, even if it wanted to, miss a single mass.
It attends the confessions of the adulterous and the wretched,
counts signatures on petitions
against abortion and same-sex marriage,
cringes at the sight of national symbols,
remembers the past as if it was yesterday,
tourists take selfies in front of it,
it shivers with cold, fear, doubt, faith,
it falls in love, falls out of love,
at the musical evenings in its honour
either it turns over in its niche
or sighs blissfully,
lulls itself to sleep under the sounds of the organ
and lapses into insomnia in the face of historic changes,
in the eternal hide-and-seek with God,
now God can't find it, now it can't find God,
before the end of every mass
the priest says "Go in peace",
and the believers hurrying to the doors chant
"Thanks be to God".
Then Chopin's heart wants to get out too,
at all costs, through the emergency exit,
or through the crack in the arch,
but a head can't knock down walls let alone a heart,
so trapped in the church pillar
its muteness makes it struggle for breath, it skips beats,
and I fear it won't be able to hold out and,
trapped between the priest and the believers,

it will have a heart attack
in front of them all.

Echo

Under the primordial house
the echo was returning from this world,
flying over the quince, the strings of tobacco leaves
and the brandy in the cauldron,
bringing us greetings from our nearest and dearest.
We were all alive then.
The bladder of the slaughtered piglets
was the toughest ball in the world,
the soup made from the old cockerel
was refused even by the hogs,
at the bottom of the soap pot
a rainbow would suddenly appear.
The cultures of the world rang out
on Macedonian Radio, Third Programme,
in the room filled with the smell of baked pumpkin
and socks drying above the stove,
where Grannie knitted a woollen waistcoat for me,
suitable for all seasons of the year.
When I outgrew it I left for the world
and lived in it in black and white,
mixing blood with water –
I didn't notice when it turned to spit,
just like the primordial house,
which was first a home,
then a property with a tax rate,
and eventually a ruin in a lawsuit.
Now we shout and shout under the house,
and the echo returns from the world beyond,
flying over the graves and dung heaps,
bringing us greetings from ourselves.

Asylum Seekers

The biggest asylum seekers' centre is under the ground.
It's the suicides, the migrants to the other world,
unaccepted, repressed and tortured in this.
The underground asylum seekers' centre offers freedom of
                                                                movement
from the periphery to the centre and vice versa,
three meals a day and a daily pass for a walk.
Asylum seekers have a standard size tag on their wristbands.
But look, the ordinary dead go on hunger strike
against the surplus of suicides around them.
They don't want asylum seekers next to their neat homes,
they don't want scattered nooses, empty pill bottles,
bones broken from falling and bellies swollen from drowning.
Instead of scarecrows they plant crosses in their green gardens
for those who died against God's will. The asylum seekers
are confused and angry, with one foot dragging backwards all
                                                                  the time.
Some have forgotten to leave a message, others to kiss their
                                                                  daughter,
some have left a suit at the dry cleaner's, others haven't made
                                                                  their wills,
some haven't cancelled their journeys, others not made an
                                                          appointment with Death.
And now they are here. With interpreters in the corridor
and folders in their hands they wait to be seen by the asylum
                                                                      officer.
Nationality, sex, religion. Many have fathers,
but no fatherland. Some are allergic to ploughed land
and, unable to kiss their soil, had to depart under the ground.
Some were life-long fugitives from themselves,

with no one to pay for pills to stop them ageing.
Some have squandered their misfortune, too, not only their
                                good fortune.
Others have not made love to the love of their life for years.
Some have been killed by their nearest and dearest, not with a
                                knife but a needle or forceps.
Among them are people who are alive only after they are dead.
The asylum seekers' centre is full, fenced off with barbed wire
from the world of the ordinary dead.

I arrived yesterday. Got two passes.
During the day I'll be in the asylum seekers' centre,
and at night in the home of the ordinary dead.
I don't know which I won't come back from.

Punctuation of Life

> *Those who don't remember me*
> *would make a city.*
> Joseph Brodsky, "Epilogue"

Home.
Fatherland.
Language.
Family tree.
Individual and collective memory.
Archetypes.
Atavism.
Uniqueness.
Ah, errata.

Home?
"Fatherland"
Language!
Family tree;
Individual and collective memory.
Archetypes –
Atavism:
Uniqueness.

Complaint.

Those who don't remember me, Joseph,
would make not one but three cities,
except the citizens have either died or moved away.
Now we meet in front of the immigration desks
at the border of the earthly, or the heavenly kingdom.

One alien is akin to another,
so we all fill in the forms together
passing the same pen from one to another.
It's only the punctuation of life
that we all, covering the form with our hand,
write
for ourselves.

from BOUNDARY SITUATION

I. BETWEEN TOMORROW AND YESTERDAY

The Past Indefinite

Life is everything that happens
between tomorrow and yesterday.
My grandmother with big pans of water
opening the door with her elbow
and closing it with her knee,
so the room, the bread, the hope don't get cold.
My grandfather curled up like a baby on the bed
after a day as long as a year in barren fields
in stifling heat which freezes his blood.
My uncle carrying on his black bicycle
the small suitcase with its historical -isms
on which I draw seductive girls
to spur him on to finish his studies sooner.
One of my aunts working three shifts in the mill
grinding away the work hours
with bags under her eyes like the little coffee cups
she bought me to play with on my own,
the other aunt hurrying towards the shoe factory
with plastic bags over her boots in the Skopje winters,
estimating the liquidation of her body with her broken boot zipper
and the liquidation of her soul with her torn boot strap.
My mother at her typewriter archiving
my early poems along with the car tyres,
while someone adds "doesn't" to the slogan
written on the city underpass entrance
saying that Auto Tyre wishes us welcome.
My father, his face stuck to the window
of the factory bus like a child in an orphanage,
curses, to hell with this life,
but even with the odd quiet moment, hell is still hell.
My sister, jaundice in the whites of her eyes,

throws up the herbal medicine the neighbour
pressed into my hands on my way back from school,
now crammed with people flooded out
by 980 cubic metres of river water per second.
I water the flowers on the balcony,
wipe the lemon and ficus tree leaves
resolutely whispering to them "One day I'm going to leave this
                                                                                              place."
Now their life is at zero distance
from today to today. I'm no longer its witness,
and neither is it mine.
When I hear someone's died
I ask what happened to them.
Nothing happens to the others in my presence any more,
in my absence everything happens to them.
Now even the most ordinary present tense for me
is nothing but past indefinite.

The Watch

When he was six
he wrote to Santa
asking him for a wristwatch.

After his father's death
he found the letter
among the old photos.

Santa had brought him
an encyclopaedia with a faded cover
listing sixty questions about time.

He had forgotten about that letter,
but for years kept collecting
wristwatches.

His children play with them –
a watch repairer's, a jeweller's,
an antiques shop.

He doesn't get mad. He winds them up,
polishes them, puts them in their boxes,
counts them and listens to their ticking.

And every night he wakes with a start
at the moment when their hands stop
to pay respects to the watch which isn't there.

Suitcases

In the little chest under my mother's bed,
brought from the village to the town,
fish-shaped dishes lay dormant for years,
each individually wrapped in newspaper,
a wedding gift, the souvenir of a society.
Their gills had gone pale, their sea grey,
when we opened the little chest
they had already eaten each other up.

In the small suitcase under my uncle's bed,
which I used to open a hundred times a day,
all the wars from all times were mixed up together
in the notes taken during history lectures.
Folded in two, in two columns,
they charged out of the trenches
towards what would later become a state,
a political suitcase of oblivion.

In the suitcase under my bed in the student dorm
I kept the Liubinka typewriter
on which the Mongolian girls, my roommates,
wrote their love letters in Cyrillic,
and before sending them across three seas,
kept them for nine nights in vodka,
in bottles with sheep guts,
the umbilical cord to their motherland.

The suitcases in Auschwitz, separated by glass
from the reach of visitors,
confiscated at the very entrance

under the arch saying Arbeit Macht Frei,
are heavy with the emptiness in which
the weight of life, the lightness of death sit hunched over.
The Holocaust was a one-way ticket from a world which vanished
in the false bottom of existence.

Life is a puff of wind among people,
leaving their suitcases in its wake.
In them knowledge gathers dust,
memory – mould, oblivion – stench.
Every suitcase is an open story,
every story is a closed suitcase.
And you don't need to leave in order to stay,
or stay to have already left.

Behind the Dead

Behind the dead linger
a guilty conscience,

mistakes, rebukes,
disputes unresolved,

promises unkept,
questions unanswered,

rifts, doubts,
pain and longings,

conflicting opinions,
ideological rubbish dumps,

a morsel of contempt and some lies,
a bubble of love and a lump of sorrow,

awakening into a dream or into a nightmare,
a cry in the night, a bad day,

the regret that we didn't
see more of each other,

the awareness that
we should have talked more,

attention never fully paid,
time unshared,

the day we last met,
the hour of the last call,

the number in the phonebook,
the book never returned,

closeness turned into alienation,
dream and reality, the unforgettable.

Behind the dead lingers
the life that ceases to be,

but in our life it
leaves death in its debt.

Emptiness

The owner of the house
of glass and bricks has died.
In the garden stand forlorn
the helicopter under the tarpaulin,
the motorbike leaning on the fence,
the two hens curled up,
one here, one there, and the rooster,
waking up only himself,
(emptiness, emptiness)
wondering
what he's still doing here.

An image crosses his mind,
of street prostitutes
warming themselves by a fire
while the clients in cars
drive in circles round them
pushing hard on the accelerator,
and he and the hens
fly above them towards death.
Emptiness, emptiness.
The owner didn't get to cut his head off,
but the rooster can no longer feel
his own head.

Women Customs Officers

I brought you some raisin cake
for the soul of my brother.
I'm not beautiful, am I?
But my sister turned even uglier
after the funeral.
Only she's a painter
and paints beautiful people.
And I came to be trained
to become a customs officer, same as you.
My village is on the border,
and now that my brother's dead,
I, too, am given priority in this country.

Puzzled, we watched her from our bunk beds
in the frontier-town boarding school
as she took the cake out
of the battered bag,
but we didn't move. *Take some*, she said
with torn-off pieces in her outstretched hands,
standing on the stepladders
and bending over between the bunks.
We all took a piece, half-heartedly,
each one of us trying to stick it somewhere,
turning to the wall,
pretending to be eating it.

Children don't eat the food for the souls –
hide the sweets in your pocket,
my granny would whisper to me
at the village graveyard gates.

And my brother would search me
on the very doorstep,
while I fought him shouting
The sweets aren't mine!
and he would throw them up in the air, victoriously,
as if he'd found drugs hidden up someone's arse,
or an antique coin in someone's bra,
or a gas pistol in a car tyre.

And now we, customs officers in training,
fend off: *The cake's not mine!*
while she hastily searches us,
and when she finds all the pieces
of the cake for the soul,
she'll confiscate our shame,
she'll issue us the highest penalty
and report us for hiding
a unique foodstuff
subjected to duty in life,
and declared duty-free in death
only by a declaration in writing.

Do You Feel Dizzy?

In a horse-drawn cart
a child, made drunk on beer,
is being taken to his circumcision.
Smirking relatives
in the street, in the mud,
play, sing, make merry.
I came across them on my way back
from the shop. He's my age,
in the same class.
When we have gym
he can't jump over the horse,
he feels dizzy and sick
even before he starts running.
Out of habit we ask him
if he feels dizzy
even when we fly paper planes
in the classroom.
And now, as he sways drunk
amidst flowers and balloons
in the horse-drawn cart,
I run over to him shouting:
Do you feel dizzy?
His head drops to his chest
the neighbourhood follows him dancing
and shouting: *Mashallah! Mashallah!*
At school, the next day,
he snores like some old drunk,
and the smell of beer spreads round him.
The teacher grabs him by the ear
and drags him to the corner.

He wobbles as he fights her off,
and the question hisses around:
Do you feel dizzy?
He feels dizzy, I say to myself, he does,
as I take a peep at him
shifting from one foot to another,
not allowed to lie down on the floor.
In gym
he suddenly dashes and jumps
over the horse. "Don't you feel dizzy?"
wonders the teacher.
"Not any more," he replies, "now I'm a man."
Everybody laughs, and
I feel my cheeks going red.
The next morning he leaves with his uncle
to work abroad,
and for a long time after that
we learn about all the things life will bring us
until it goes dizzy with us,
or we with it.

Plus-minus

Once I could count the dead
on the fingers of one hand,
now they are too many to count.

Once I could count the living
to make me fall asleep,
now I repeat the few names over and over again.

If the thought crosses my mind
that a person might die,
I'm immediately nicer to them.

Amazing how easy it is
to be nice
to potentially dead people!

But as soon as dying
is postponed,
living gets postponed as well.

And then
the body loses time,
the soul gets it.

The body leaves the space,
the soul inhabits it,
the spirit displaces it.

Between the dead and the living
the difference is a plus-minus,
a degree or two in temperature:

the former have got colder,
the latter have got burnt,
and all of them (n)either alive (n)or dead.

II. CRUMBLING

The Crumbling House

... should be euthanised as quickly as possible,
the water, electricity and gas turned off,

the TV, telephone, router sealed,
all electrical appliances unplugged from their sockets,

the IV drip ripped out
and the shutters barred for the last time,

then the bulldozer is given the nod
and goodbye house, once a home – goodbye home, not even a
                                                        house any more.

It should be buried in the hollow of its own foundations,
and visited on All Souls Day with offerings and candles,

and time, they say, will gradually heal the pain.
But what if it has decided to flee its fate itself?

You get a call saying it ran out into the road, but all trace of it is lost,
like a demented old woman it wandered off who knows where,

you'll report it missing, put up a poster on the broken fence,
and nobody will ever find it either alive or dead.

The Crumbling Memory

...should be swallowed in the rumen of your consciousness
and in a sleepless night regurgitated back into your mouth,

and then chewed, and re-chewed till the morning
with focused jaw movements like the steps of a tightrope walker,

to ruminate like the sheep in East Macedonia
chewed the cud in the dead silence of the house barn

while Grannie was dragging you to the outhouse half-asleep in
                                                                    wet pyjamas
and their teeth smacked through the juices of the pastures,

just like your teeth now smack through the water of oblivion
picking up here and there a random souvenir of yourself.

Soaked with the spittle of the soul, memory should be
swallowed atom by atom, decomposing itself into a force

to pull your body out of the well of the subconscious
until life uses its nutritional value

as best it can, for memory is food,
without which you thin, fall sick, if underfed you die,

without memory you decay as it decays.
Humans are ruminants with a rumen – a soul

and a stomach – a spirit, and into them the crumbling memory,
as if flowing from one cup into another,

should be poured and left to overflow
until it becomes itself a body from its own cell.

The Crumbling Country

... should be left head over heels,
just grab the language, the passport and some photos,

stuff birth, childhood, youth, life,
into a child's rucksack

and, head bowed, start on the road to exile.
Your legs move of their own accord, led by collective memory,

escaping is your heritage, statutory succession
from the fatherland, your ancestors' physical fitness.

You have to cross the border curled up in a car boot
at the moment when the flag is lowered to half mast,

and then, barefoot, hungry and with a kick up the arse
walk away from it step by step for months

from the human in the other towards the human in yourself.
When *homo politicus* kills, the suicide is both the executioner
                                                         and the victim.

You'll leave the crumbling country
never batting an eyelid while your soul blinks and howls

like the revolving light and siren of the police patrol car
which you hope will catch you

and have you sent back,
but it vanishes in the distance.

The Crumbling History

...should be reburied, like reburying in the liberated area
the bones of those killed in occupied territory,

it should be unearthed like the conscience of the murderers,
and the survivors should be ghettoised

to talk to themselves in a language
incomprehensible to the dead.

In crumbling history you become thick-skinned,
nothing touches you any more,

and it's only through the mucous membrane that sometimes
the misfortune evaded reaches you

like when your feet, size 36, neither children's nor women's,
disappeared into your father's military boots, size 43,

part of the equipment of the Yugoslav reservists.
Alternative lifestyle - your feet in shoes as big as shovels.

In both the previous and the next war
the same thud, statutory death, and life a war game.

Two out of eleven children survived
and, of you two, neither had a child.

They shovelled soil on some of them,
on others they stamped it down with their boots,

and yet others sprinkled it on themselves.
Instead of a cross, history is crucified over the graves.

Decades later death is the DNA of life,
but life will never again be the DNA of death.

Your father returned the boots to the military unit,
you never returned to where it should not have happened again,

that crumbling history, buried in the mass grave
that you should find and dig up, to your own cost.

The Crumbling Future

...should be turned upside down like a stool with its legs up
in a freshly swept and mopped jazz club in Chicago

with a For Sale sign on the door through which went the waitress,
without her night pay, not to go to bed but to catch the first train

to the nursing home where the end of the future lies,
even though everyone believed in it all last night. But not her,

while she was guessing, in some Eastern European language,
what it was the sax player with black skin under the white shirt

had been beaten with when he was a child?
With a belt, as her father had beaten her – so that she'd see a
                                                       shooting star,

or with a birch, as her teacher had beaten her – so as she'd touch it,
or with the palm of the hand, as she was beaten by her husband –
                                                       to snuff it out?

The saxophone split the air like the trumpet of the Roma player
at the wedding in her forefathers' small village,

where the first intercourse was determined strictly geographically,
and only became a political act when she left.

She dropped the glasses, the owner lost his temper,
the present on shaky legs ended without a past.

The crumbling future should go up as the barrier does
once you've paid your parking ticket,

but the attendant is nowhere to be seen and the barrier
                                                        doesn't go up,
and you realise that life isn't a car park

from which the driver has walked away, clutching the parking
                                                                                ticket
smeared with sweat and tears, expired forever.

The Crumbling World

... should be wrapped up in a hospital sheet
and transferred on a stretcher to the palliative care unit

where life expectancy is six months at most,
dignified and peaceful dying with pain control.

The window is open, the room is just for one,
pigeons cooing in the garden, lilacs on the small table.

Like in a restaurant kitchen, the sign above the door to the room
says "Smile" and all those coming in to visit

have a grin on their faces, although no one feels like laughing
and prefers the coalminers' "Good Luck" before the pit of death.

The smell of ammonia and iodine, of mandarin and banana peel,
evening news on the radio about new wars and financial crises

which don't affect the patient any more. But it hurts. In a corner
of its conscience
the world knows: even its beauty couldn't save it, and in vain did
the poets

want to change it. And suddenly it feels between the bones and
the skin
an amorous craving: for at least one more chance to make love to
freedom

which waves to it from the door: "Sleep, I'll drop by when I can."
The crumbling world should be left

in the hospice where the angels of life have no intention of either speeding up or delaying its death.

III. A HUMAN OR HUMANKIND?

The Pet

She offers him powdered milk and he wants the milk of a grandame,
she feeds him mashed fruit and he wants mashed blood and soil,
she bathes him in the baby bath with natural baby soap
and he wants hallowed water blessed by an archbishop,
she dries him with a cotton towel
and he wants the flag from the trunk in the Archives,
she wraps him in a blanket covered with bear cubs
and he wants a vintage woollen shag rug,
she puts him in a cot with a canopy of stars,
and he wants a cradle with swastikas,
she lulls him to sleep with tales from Andersen and Grimm
and he wants local legends of victories without defeats,
she wakes him up with a children's rhyme
and he wants an anthem withdrawn from use,
she dresses him in brightly coloured playsuits
and he wants a black uniform,
she puts light shoes on his feet
and he wants steel-toed studded army boots,
she hands him a little ball with rainbow arches
and he wants a baseball bat with a skull and crossbones,
she teaches him to play Ludo on the garden bench
and he wants to weave barbed wire for the border,
she lets him play in the sand with the other children
and he pinches them if their skin is a different colour,
she holds him by his left hand when they go for a walk
and he stretches out his right and marches,
she puts hay fever drops in his eyes
and he wants antihistamine for otherness,
she teaches him foreign languages to enrich him
and he spits at her in his language he doesn't even speak properly,

she teaches him good, and he loves evil,
she takes him to history class and he repeats history,
she gives him a dog – puppy dog
she buys him a cat – kitty cat
and he punches her eye out of its socket,
spits in her face and screams:
I'm Nazi! Nazi, Nazi!

Traduttore, traditore

No, there was most certainly no God then,
or He was clinically dead,
I tell myself in Auschwitz, and she
in front of the prefab where twenty thousand Roma ended up,
tells me: "This is where they finished off the Gypsies."
The rain is pouring down in four dimensions.
Our nylon rain capes are allies with the rain drops.
I walk beside her, trying to get away from her.
I enter every prefab, I read all the captions,
stare at all the photographs.
"It's all in the books, we don't need to look at everything,"
she says, and her age, older than Auschwitz,
flounders before the stairs,
but not before the words.
I leave her in the lanes swimming in mud,
I forget about her among the reflections of evil.
She waits for me in the rain at the corner of the gas chamber,
asking a young guide if she knows
where her uncle was killed in 1942.
Maybe she is human after all, I say to myself,
one torn apart by the pains of those I never knew,
and I can't make out if the one I know hurts her too.

That evening in the hotel room we drink linden tea,
me silent out of stubbornness, sadness and anger,
she letting little snakes out of her mouth:
she can't abide women and their human rights,
she can't abide taxi drivers with foreign accents,
she can't abide artists ridiculing the government,
she can't abide homosexuals, lesbians,

well, in this world, she says, there are only men, women, and
                                               families,
she can't abide Europe – only her country's government is good,
and not one single member of her nation ever betrayed a
                                              neighbour.
And indeed, she says, it's a crime to say anything different.
I listen to her, with my palms sweating and my body oozing
the last raindrops of the day in Auschwitz,
my head begins to feel as heavy as a rock,
but that's fine, let it be even heavier
so that I cannot raise it abruptly
and in a fog of frenzy
shut her mouth with the pillow,
to kill the little snakes falling out of it,
for doesn't evil beget evil,
and isn't everything bad good for something?
God, you who are not, you who are,
but who was obviously not in Auschwitz,
should know that yourself.
Or you too are *traduttore, traditore,*
literally, down to the bone?

A Curse

May you be eaten by Paradise! was Father Kleopa's
curse on me. Steep was the ground
from his skete to the foot of the hill where I stood.

The curses our people use have always been hellish:
"May your heart eat you, may you never see the light of day."
I was stumbling downward, crawling upward.

Guts upside down, scratched and out of breath,
I entered the first church I came across. The priest
had just recited the Creed,

and a child shouted: "Blavo!" clapping its little hands.
Muffled laughter. Older women in a scolding voice:
"You don't say bravo in church!"

The priest thundered: "Not even here do you respect God,
still less at home – wining and dining
like at the Last Supper!"

And the mother with the child, hurrying to the exit, whispered:
"If you live in hell, you'll be wined and dined in heaven."
I left the church. And followed her.

A Human or Humankind?

To love the man who spits on the ground
next to you at the traffic lights,
or the drunkard sprawled in front of the kiosk,
stinking and swearing at the passersby not giving him coins,
or the woman who pummels a child who's wetted his pants
as if he's a punch bag,
or the child lying on the floor in the shop
and kicking his granny,
or the boy who snatched a passenger's purse
and vanished in the blink of an eye,
or the policeman who's just pocketed the money
and thrown away the driver's breathalyser,
or the neighbour who deliberately emptied her ashtray
on the clothes drying on your balcony,
or the driver who sprayed you with mud head to toe
driving 200 km an hour close to the pavement,
or the hypocrite kneeling in God's temple
who falls asleep hating her own sister,
or the maniac who rubs up against you in the bus,
or the politician who washes your brain
at the highest possible temperature,
or the prison guard who takes it out
on pregnant inmates,
or the president of the young right-wingers
who threatens migrant children,
or the woman who abducts little girls for human trafficking,
or the dictator who's put his own needs above those of his country
or the soldier who smashes with his buttstock
the baby sucking at its mother's breast,
or the serial killer, the paedophile, the rapist,

the juvenile delinquent, the war criminal,
the friend who became your foe,
or that man, that woman, those people
who've been abusing, humiliating, destroying
since the beginning of the world,
to love everyone as you love yourself,
and yourself, too, as you love them
- but how, how?

And humankind is so easy to love.
Humankind is nice company
to sit with for a cup of coffee,
free from the burden weighing on a human,
and goes its own way to its destination,
not having to walk over dead bodies
for a human has already trampled down the others.
Every human is guilty of something,
but not so humankind,
a human is transient, humankind eternal,
humankind is honest and perfect,
a human the opposite,
so how can you love an imperfect individual
amid the perfect multitude?
It's easier to love humankind,
when the human beside you isn't worthy of love,
but you have to obey the commandment
to love thy neighbour as thyself,
and you don't know which is more of a neighbour to you,
a human or humankind?

The (Dis)comfort of Existence

Why is neither God nor love,
nor life nor country
              comfortable
like an armchair with a footstool,
like the seat in business class
with an eye mask and scented blanket,
like a bathtub with rose leaves
and ripples of aromatic oils?

Why are God and love
and life and country
              uncomfortable
like a sleeping bag on a shingle beach
like a wooden seat in a Proleter bus
like a poorly inflated air mattress,
like a three-legged stool in a shadeless garden,
like a tight shoe?

Don't ask the faithful or loved ones,
or the living or those with homes,
but ask those that are not such and they'll tell you
that you enter eternal themes
through the back door,
and leave through the front door,
with your head back, your legs forward,
and arms hanging in the emptiness.

God and love
and life and country
justify their existence only when

in art they have an unhappy end,
and in death a happy one.
And existence is (dis)comfort
and the beginning of all that has never been
or shall ever be.

Whose Are You?

Whose are you, children? Grandpa would ask us
when our paths crossed at the village water tap.

Whose? Well, yours! We'd laugh, water on our cheeks,
and Grandpa would look at us doubtfully and shake his head.

Only at home did he not ask us that,
only at home did he recognise us.

Beyond the threshold we were someone's children, but whose,
                                                                                     whose?
He's got sunstroke, Grannie would say,

he's got old, my uncle would add, how can he remember you?
But Grandpa hadn't recognised us outside even when we were
                                                                                     little,

since that night when the Virgin led him back home through
                                                                      the darkness,
together with the sheep lost on the mountain. A living icon,

he kept saying for years, though Grannie kept warning him
not to say it in front of other people – these are pagan times.

Whose are you, Grandpa? we asked him one day
when our paths crossed near the barn.

Whose? Well, yours! He smiled unconvincingly, looking at the
                                                                          cows.
And we stared, unconvincingly, in the same direction.

Beyond the threshold he was someone's grandpa, but whose,
                                                    whose?
One faith suddenly wiped out the world before his eyes,

before old age mowed him down he was hit
by the hand of the village secret agent in a leather coat,

which long afterwards spread stench throughout the graveyard
to which my grandpa was taken too, a living icon.

Cleaning

How is David to be cleaned?
Should he be rubbed with a soft toothbrush,
or soaped with Palmolive?
Or bathed like a baby,
fingers clenched around his shoulder?

And what about the head of Nefertiti in eco paint
nodding from the traffic lights before the Iron Curtain?
Should the barefoot orphans who wipe the windscreens
with their brushes on long handles
be called in to help?

Should Rodin's Thinker
be wiped with a wool cloth heavy with vinegar,
lemon juice, or baking soda,
and then polished with a lens wipe,
head to toe? Or just a shower would do?

As for Degas' Little Dancer Aged Fourteen
my mother would rub her with bleach
and then starch her tutu,
not knowing that it's politically incorrect,
but conceptually well-founded.

The Venus de Milo
requires special care
and use of biocosmetics only,
and there's no question of a sauna
in case she sweats and loses weight.

And Michelangelo's Pietà,
can she even be touched
for fear of smearing her with human hygiene?
Cleaning is the fruit of death,
a three-day mourning of life, dust to dust.

And in the end it's your turn –
but how can you clean your own skin?
Washing it with soap and water is pointless
if under it there are rusty layers of all that
you shouldn't have been – but could have, could have.

Means of Transport

I locked Him to a bike rack
and ran off to work.
I kept repeating the combination numbers to myself
but once I'd gone inside they vanished from my head.
That afternoon I went back
and tried to release Him
but no combination
worked on the lock.
I tugged Him, shook Him,
implored Him to answer my pleas
and unlock Himself,
I beseeched both His mother and all the saints
to show mercy
on me and on Him,
and shatter the chain
- slavery and freedom in one,
but nothing.
God remained fastened
to the bike rack.
Alone – all the stands were now empty.
I could hardly drag myself home
and the next morning shouldered pliers and keys,
determined to release God
at any cost.
And when I got there, He was gone,
the bike stand, too, as if it had never been there.
An empty space between two bikes
overgrown with grass.
Someone had taken Him away along with everything else,
someone had stolen God from me,

along with the silver lock
and the forgotten code
of a hundred thousand combinations,
my means of transport
from earth to heaven
my *Premium*-bike God,
gone to hell.

The Evil

Evil, says Dr. Gerhard Roth,
> *"lurks in the central lobe of the brain,*
> *and is visible on a scanner*
> *as a dark mass"*
>> (Filip David, "The House of Memory and Oblivion")

Like a stomach ulcer,
kidney stones,
a metastasis spreading
to the edges of the body.
Like the red-hot poker in the hand
of a boy returning to his snowman
to make a hole in its heart
while his mother yells at him
Mind you don't burn your jacket!
Like the trackers of the last descendants
of the northern white rhino
watched over in the middle of the savanna
by four guards with rifles
- evolution can be slept through,
but not poachers.
Like the nanny
who got bored by the baby,
the unending twinkle twinkle, itsy bitsy,
baa, baa black sheep,
so now she pinches it with her icy nails
to make it stop crying.
Like the race, the nation, the religion
locking a cattle truck
full of half-alive people, repeating
that they were just doing their job,

evil is a dark mass,
a body without soul hiding
in your centremost part
that only when another dies
can itself live.

History

Dead people in living years,
living people in dead years.

Dead peoples in living decades,
living peoples in dead decades.

Dead humanities in living centuries,
living humanities in dead centuries.

Each time has unwanted histories,
each history unwanted times.

With its content, summary and key words,
history is a paper on life and death.

After the conference it will be duly published in the proceedings,
which no one will ever read.